Poems & Depression

Honest Poetry of Depression and Hope

Javin Stanley

Copyright © 2019 Javin Stanley

All rights reserved. No part of this publication may be reproduced, stored in or introduced into a retrieval system, or transmitted in any form or by any means without the prior written consent of the copyright holder.

Book cover and artwork by Sabrina Carnes.

Author photo by Jacob Rewerts.

ISBN: 978-0-578-50686-9

DEDICATION

This book is dedicated to everyone who has and is battling depression. From one soul who deals with depression to another; may you find comfort in knowing you aren't alone in this battle and may you find strength and hope to keep going on.

CONTENTS

Introduction	i

**Part One
The Dark Side:
The Way it Is**

Poems of Depression	1
Depressing Monoryhmes	7
The ABCs of Depression	13
Terza Rima Depresso	19
Elegy's Depression	25

**Part Two
The Light Side:
The Way it Can Be**

Poems of Hope	34
Hopeful Sonnets	40
Acrostic's Hope	46
Quatrain's Hopeful	52
Hope's Free Verse	58
Conclusion	65

INTRODUCTION

WARNING: All of the depressing poems are brutally honest and may cause some of you to feel overwhelmed. If you find yourself in that state, please feel free to stop reading for a bit or skip ahead to the hopeful poems until you feel comfortable continuing.

Part One

The Dark Side: The Way it Is

Poems of Depression

Endless Darkness

Is there any way out,
Of this endless hole?
A path to the light.
A victory untold.
Cuz' I can't stand,
My hopeless soul.
And it's ongoing torture,
A tale of woe.

My Worth

I wonder if they meant,
To hurt me so much.
To the point where I,
Lost my crutch.
My guess is they did,
I mean why would they not?
I'm just not worth it.
No not another shot.
Nothing I've done,
Or that I'll ever do,
Will measure up to anything.
Especially not for you.

Hidden Pain

I can't tell anyone,
Not a single soul.
Of how I really feel,
This mind taking a toll.
From all the dark thoughts,
And all of the chatter,
That goes on in my brain,
Those thoughts I can't shatter.
I know they won't get it,
The pain I go through.
I'm the only one who's felt it.
That I know is true.

Unhappy Loophole

Why is it whenever,
I finally feel happy?
That my life starts to sink,
Again, it turns crappy?
It's like I can't win,
No matter what.
I try my hardest,
But I always get stuck.
Inside this pitfall,
That I can't escape.
I climb to the top,
Only to be greeted by a gate.
A gate with no key,
A gate with no lock.
A gate that won't open,
So trying I will stop.

Real Questions

When I'm gone will it matter?
Will they care that I disappeared?
Is it important that I'm here?
Is death something that should be feared?
Am I worth anything?
Am I really ever needed?
Do I even deserve to breathe?
Just a garden never weeded?
A human without a purpose?
A human that won't be missed?
Someone who shouldn't live?
Someone who should cease to exist?

JAVIN STANLEY

Depressing Monorhymes

The Dragging Years

One year, two years, three years five.
How many depressed years can I survive?
I've been holding on, for so long.
How have my fingers not yet, slipped and gone?
Someday soon, I hope I go.
For these dragging years, turned me hollow.

One step, two steps, three steps five.
How many tired steps before I dive?
Right into, this unforgiving pool.
Where all my demons, begin to drool.
Over my body and over my mind,
Preparing for the day that they can dine.

I've Tried

I've tried to be good, at everything.
I took my bat and took a swing.
At being perfect, at being great.
But all I ended up with, was hate.
Hate for myself, hate for you.
For making me feel worthless and blue.

Because whatever I tried was never enough.
You always said I wasn't tough.
I tried my best and always checked,
To make sure to earn your respect.
But your standards are too high.
Still, I will believe all your lies.

Failure Road

Failing my classes and failing my grades.
I'm looking forward to better days.
Losing jobs and losing friends.
Will I ever meet my ends?
Missing faith and all hope.
Alcohol is how I cope.
With all my failures on my back,
Drinking 'til my vision's black.
There's no other way, I can stand.
This pathetic life I somehow spanned.

Facade

Fake smiles and fake faces.
Just enough to get me places.
Fake emotions, fake expressions.
I need them to avoid the questions.
Fake actions and fake happiness.
Used only to hide my darkness.

No Love

I don't think I've ever felt love.
They all must have felt above.
Showing some affection,
Making a connection.
A kind gesture, a kind word.
Something that I never heard.

A simple hug would have been nice.
But giving a hug they never thought twice.
Always at arm's length.
Never receiving strength.
Left on my own.
Love, never shown.

JAVIN STANLEY

The ABC'S of Depression

Low

What a downer
Xylophone's low pitch
Yacht sinking
Zero cloud nine
I feel lower than a buried casket.

Struggling

Struggling child
Tired soul
Undone progress
View blurred
My endless challenges will end me.

Alone

Lonely nights
Made up friends
No one around
Only myself
The one soul I know is my own.

Bad Habit

Grown man
Hazardous habits
Insidious lies
Jack and cokes
Drinking heavily is my only escape.

Black Rose

A dead flower
Black rose lain
Colored after death
Dark intentions made
The flower that represents my soul.

JAVIN STANLEY

Terza Rima Depresso

Nobody's There

Why did dad leave, why does mom drink?
Why does my family hate me?
These things I can't help but think.

The bullies at school, won't let me be.
They shove me to the ground, calling me names.
I tell the teachers, their offices they make me flee.

I tell my friends I'm depressed, "we're tired of your games".
They say with their annoyed faces.
Not believing a single one of my claims.

"No one cares", I say untying my laces.
I climb into bed with a trail of tears.
As I lay there, my mind goes places.

And the thing that really grinds my gears,
Is the fact that I trusted them for years.

Sad Boy/Sad Girl

I'm just a sad boy,
Who can't seem to be happy.
So I guess I'll dismiss my ploy.

Everyday feels crappy,
Stuck in a swirl.
I suppose forever I will be unhappy.

I'm just a sad girl,
Who feels more than sad.
I look in the mirror, and wanna hurl.

I just wish I could be glad.
For this life that is mine.
But I consistently feel bad.

I'm just a sad boy whose life is a staggering line.
I'm just a sad girl who's drinking too much wine.

Prevented Life

My depression is keeping me from living life.
From inspiration, from motivation.
From moving forward, away from this strife.

All of this contemplation,
Is driving me insane.
It's staining my soul with frustration.

I'm starting to feel so inane.
Thinking this plan was my saving grace.
That my broken heart, I could maintain.

"Is this all just a pointless race?"
I say as I fell.
With my hands on my head, tears leaving my face.

And I go back to those thoughts that I know so damn well.
As I once again go through, another day of hell.

Dead Emotions

My feelings are dead.
Goodbye emotions.
I stared blankly as they bled.

Going through the motions.
A robot through and through.
Can't fix this with any magic potions.

Who would have known.
That my heart would go numb.
Something I did not condone.

I'd say I feel like scum.
But I can't feel at all.
No longer a beat to this drum.

I'd smile now, but there's a stall.
Because all my emotions have left me AWOL.

Where Was God?

Where were you God?
I prayed every day.
Are you nothing but a fraud?

I needed you, to take this pain away.
This pain that aches my soul.
My faith is starting to sway.

Because every time I stroll,
Calling out Your name.
I never feel whole.

All of my prayers are the same.
Just as they are ignored.
You are the one I will blame.

So I yell skyward,
And curse Your name from my knees.
Swearing, "You'll never be my lord".

Shaking my fists as they squeeze.
I throw my bible in a fire.
I guess You just do as You please.

You left me alone when I was dire.
From now on I shall welcome hellfire.

JAVIN STANLEY

Elegy's Depression

Lost Son

We never saw this coming.
We all thought he was fine.
Didn't know he was running.
From pain all his life.

Chills run down my spine.
As I clean that bloodstained knife.
How could I have missed the sign?
That death, his life would soon see.

Oh child, we will miss you.
Our seemingly happy son.
If we had known what you were going through,
We surely would have helped you.

His Only Friend

I was your only friend.
The only one you trusted.
Up until the very end.
Your secrets I did keep.

All of your problems, all of your struggles.
These things to me you explained.
Along with all of your troubles,
Only to me it was known.

I wish I was, your reason to stay.
A trusted comrade, a loyal friend.
But I know pain, has a way.
Of making loved ones, seem nonexistent.

The one thing you didn't tell me.
Was that you would take pills.
Cuz' you knew that I would be,
The only one who could save you.

Hanging Girl

She had cuts on her arms.
She had cuts on her legs.
The sound of any alarm,
Something she did not dread.

My sister was bullied and bruised.
She never ate too much food.
Always felt like she was being used.
Especially on that night she was raped.

Have you ever walked in,
On a loved one hanging from the ceiling?
The pain I felt, explaining I could not begin.
But as much as it killed me, her torture I could not imagine.

Everything she went through,
Must have been hell.
For her to come to,
Such a devastating end.

Depressed Father

He was fired from his job.
Mom left him a month ago.
I watched him slowly grab the doorknob.
As he went into his empty home.

His dad never believed in him.
Like an ear to an obvious liar.
Always told him he wasn't slim.
With some sort of evil grin.

Dad never deserved it.
No not at all.
But all of those voices that wouldn't quit.
Pushed him to the edge.

My tears then were flowing.
As they soaked his broken body.
And that building that he dropped from, without knowing.
That its tall structure, would forever and always haunt me.

Goodbye

It's like bad nostalgia,
This feeling that I get.
When I'm lookin' attcha.
In that casket all dressed in black.

I look at your head,
Where the bullet flew.
Wish I was the one who was dead,
And not you.

If only I was there,
To pull your finger off the trigger.
I wouldn't be here, deep in prayer.
Asking for your revival.

I would rewind it all.
Just to see you breathe again.
My one true love, I feel so small.
Left behind, with your ring against mine.

I was so excited,
To be your wife.
But until we are reunited,
My heart will ache with strife.

Depression got the best of you.
The best of you I wish I had.
If only the last sound you knew,
Wasn't a loud, blood curling "bang!".

POEMS & DEPRESSION

Part Two

The Light side: The Way it Can Be

Poems of Hope

Let's Be Real

Here's the thing,
About that depression.
It may never completely flee.
An uncomfortable confession.
Some of you will eliminate it,
Some of you will be forced to cope.
But as long as you are breathing,
There is still hope.
Though it may not leave you forever,
Victory it will not keep.
Because you are stronger than those lies.
The circumstances that buried you deep.

Can't it Be?

If life can be dark,
Can't it also be light?
That shadow will disappear,
When life becomes bright.
Where there is a Yang,
There's certainly a Yin.
That can fight back the darkness,
Destroying its kin.
Life may suck,
That's definitely true.
But life can be good,
There are just some hoops you must jump through.

Metaphorical Weather

Before the calm,
There is a storm.
A famous saying,
A fire to keep you warm.
As you wait for blue skies,
Inside that grim cave.
Watching as it rains.
Those drops, hard to brave.
One day the sun,
Will dry up the land.
And you will smile,
As you lay on the sand.
More grey clouds will come,
But at least you know.
That the sun will be back,
And it will help you grow.

Escape the Hole

I know you fell,
Inside that hole.
And that it feels endless,
The pain of your tortured soul.
But there is a bottom,
And there is a way.
To escape that long fall,
To see the light of day.
Look for the ropes,
That have dropped down there.
And just start climbing,
Though your hands are bare.
Some ropes may snap,
And some may be frayed.
But don't look back,
And don't be afraid.
Because one of those ropes,
Will lead you right out.
Right out of that hole,
That was filled with doubt.

Like Something Hopeful

Like a bird finding its wings,
You'll find a way to soar.
Like a caterpillar becoming a butterfly,
You'll be so much more.
Like a child who learned to walk,
You'll learn how to stand your ground.
Like a determined lover,
From your failures you'll rebound.
Like a pencil at the end of a maze,
You'll make it past these walls.
Like all cartoon characters,
You can survive the waterfalls.
Like a Champion,
You will rise.
And like a colored sky,
You'll be a beautiful sunrise.

JAVIN STANLEY

Hopeful Sonnets

What You Need

Maybe you need pills.
To keep you going.
To stop the blood spills.
To hold your flowing.
Maybe you need therapy.
An outsider's point of view.
Hours of psychotherapy.
Something to get you through.
Maybe you need an outlet.
Put your pain in a song.
Write it in a booklet.
And then say "so long!"
Maybe what you need, is a trusting friend.
Who will be there for you, till the very end.

One Day

You are in your room.
Crying yourself to sleep.
Thinking of your doom.
Your body in a heap.
Why does everything go wrong?
Why can't life let me be?
Why is it hard to be strong?
These questions you can't flee.
Hopelessness you feel.
Right before you drift off.
Into sleep where you conceal.
Bad dreams that seem to scoff.
But one day you will hear good news.
And your hope will no longer have a bruise.

Out of Bed

Getting out of bed,
Can be difficult.
When your heart and your head.
Have been thrown by a catapult.
The rope cut by doubt.
The contraption made of fear.
Flying through an unknown route.
Nothing is clear.
You want to stay,
Under those covers.
Keeping the darkness at bay.
As above your head, it hovers.
But getting out of bed, is the first step.
To defeating the darkness, yourself you must rep.

Confrontation

Avoiding the facts.
In the back of your mind.
Distractions to the max.
Making yourself blind.
To something you can't admit.
Something you want to ignore.
A truth you won't permit.
To your thoughts no more.
But no longer could you hold it.
These feelings that are repressed.
As you release it your teeth grit.
You are, indeed, depressed.
Little did you know, that confronting this feeling.
Is where your true power begins, and so does your healing.

God Only Knows

Feels like God left you.
Alone in the dark.
Not a single clue.
Nor a simple remark.
To where He is.
Or why you're in pain.
Or even what His,
Plans contain.
Some say there's reason.
For the hurt you go through.
Why God put you in this season,
Something you wish you knew.
We may never know, why pain He makes us face.
But I bet we'd understand, if we saw all time and space.

JAVIN STANLEY

Acrostic's Hope

Hope

H-aving it will keep you going
O-nward you will go
P-ushing through life's pitfalls
E-nduring the pain to find a better life

Optimism

O-pen your mind
P-leasure you will find
T-hen as you see
I-nfinite possibilities
M-uch to your surprise
I-nward peace shall arrive
S-o long as you keep on
M-oving towards positive thinking

Positive

P-adlocks removed
O-ff of your brain
S-ee the bright light
I-nviting you to change
T-hinking things won't get better
I-n time they will
V-anishing doubts in sight
E-xciting this transformation is

Believe

B-egin where you are
E-ven if it's hard
L-ook to the blue sky
I-sn't it beautiful?
E-ventually your life will be clear
V-oid of grey skies
E-scalate that belief in a finer future

Gratitude

G-rateful for what you have
R-eally could be worse
A-ppreciate the good
T-hat comes with the bad
I-nvest in appreciative habits
T-ake back your happiness
U-sed to complaining
D-own to stop the groaning
E-dit those ungrateful thoughts and
  Be free

JAVIN STANLEY

Quatrain's Hopeful

Continued Life

With continued life comes new opportunities.
New beginnings and new life.
So just keep living, put down that knife.
And push back depression with newfound immunities.

Remove the Hood

Your life isn't all bad.
There's certainly some good.
Remove that dark, concealing hood.
That blocks the things that make you glad.

Care for Yourself

Show yourself some self-care.
Be kind to your heart and mind.
Though as humans to flaws we are confined.
Your well-being shouldn't be in despair.

There for You

Some people are there for you.
Whether you believe it or not.
Find the ones who are worth the shot.
And let them know what you are going through.

Sweet Tooth

Easier said than done.
Most of hope's truth.
I know giving up is your sweet tooth.
But this is a fight that can be won.

JAVIN STANLEY

Hope's Free Verse

Just Hold On

Just hold on, I know it's hard.
To keep going, and be strong.
The battle may be long.
And it might seem never ending.
But I promise you it gets better.
Even in stormy weather.
Maybe not in ways you expected.
It will creep up on you.
Like a child's game of peek-a-boo.
Suddenly life ain't so bad.
Just hold on dear, you won't regret it.

How Far You've Come

Look how far you've come,
Despite your daily struggles.
You've managed to make it through.
And all of the things that helped you become;
Stronger, smarter and braver too.
Are things that you made it through.
You've come so far, from where you were.
Those past pains can't stop you now.
Don't be sad when you look back.
Be proud of yourself and don't you worry.
For all of the progress that you have made.
Will lead you to happier days.

Laugh it Off

Laugh at your mistakes.
Oh, how funny they are.
You might not be perfect.
But that's okay by far.
Everyone messes up.
You aren't the only one.
So just chuckle when it's done.
And realize that you're alright.
Laugh at the way you failed.
Laugh at how you missed the point.
Laugh at how you used to be.
And laugh at the times when you were filled with doubt.
Because you got through it.
And you are better now than you were back then.
Sure, you messed up a bit.
But that's nothing that a laugh can't fix.

Have Hope

Have hope when it's all going wrong.
Have hope when all seems lost.
Have hope when you've hit the bottom.
Have hope when the dust is what you have bitten.
Hope is the key to survival.
Hope is your helping hand.
Hope will get you through the pain.
Hope will give you strength to regain,
The energy to fight for another day.
So that someday you will see.
That a good life is possible.
And that you can finally be happy.

This is It

This is it.
This is your time.
This is the day that you finally arrive.
Exactly where you wanted to be.
The end of your long climb.
You are happy and you are healthy.
And you are filled with joy.
This is your victory against the dark.
This is your win with a smile and a smirk.
You found the light you had when you were a boy.
You fulfilled your promise you made to that young girl in the pictures.
To be happy once again.
Man, does it feel good.
Knowing that you beat depression.
Sure, it might come back for you to restrain.
But little does depression know, that you finally have power over it.

JAVIN STANLEY

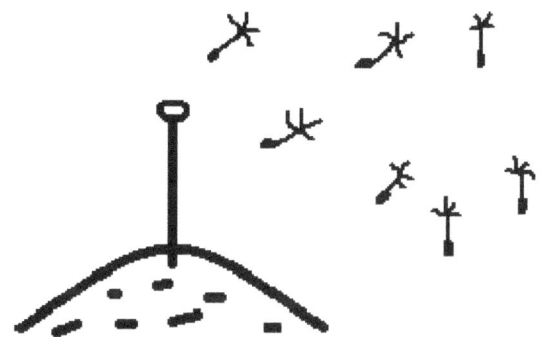

Conclusion

What is depression like?
It's like being handicapped mentally.
It feels like no one loves you, even though some people do.
It's like there's no hope for a future, when you actually have a whole lifetime ahead of you.
It's like you can't see past the here and now.
It's replaying the same old pain over and over again.
It's like being held down by an invisible force.
It feels impossible to escape.
And after all of the hurt and pain that depression has caused me, if I could describe it in one word, it would be that depression...is a liar.

JAVIN STANLEY

ABOUT THE AUTHOR

Javin Stanley is a part-time janitor and blogger. He was born and currently lives in Waverly, Iowa. During his free time, he enjoys playing video games, playing tennis, kayaking, listening to music and hanging out with his friends. He was homeschooled and is an introvert who loves self-discovery.

www.ingramcontent.com/pod-product-compliance
Lightning Source LLC
LaVergne TN
LVHW091317080426
835510LV00007B/533